Economic Solidarity Program
The Best Financial Solutions Necessary to
Provide Liquidity Material and
How to Avoid the Financial Problem
Facing Individual, Family, and Community

Economic Solidarity Program
The Best Financial Solutions Necessary to
Provide Liquidity Material and
How to Avoid the Financial Problem
Facing Individual, Family, and Community

Mohammed Hassan Alzahrani

To order additional copies of this book, contact:
Xlibris Corporation
0-800-644-6988
www.Xlibrispublishing.co.uk
Orders@Xlibrispublishing.co.uk
305555

CONTENTS

A Dedication to All People
Who Desire to Acquire Liquidity

Everyone is able to acquire 38% of his total yearly income if he uses the personal account method, within a period not later than 10 months. Such amounts acquired within 10 months equal the value of refinancing by one of the banks with which customers treat, where the bank cannot make refinancing for customers unless after one year from the date of the first financing. We conclude that this method nearly equals the amount of refinancing.

OBJECTIVES OF THE BOOK

1. To find a method suitable for maintaining the middle-class financial situation

2. Making a family members program organizes the financial issues

3. Major companies shall specify poor-class individuals to use their abilities in the execution of some projects

INTRODUCTION

Praise be upon him.

Firstly, I would like to put some solutions that can be used easily, where this version discusses some financial solutions to all the community individuals and presents the best method to acquire liquidity and get rid of financial problems as much as possible: opening a personal account or financial participation from the family and community individuals to acquire cash liquidity. As known, these days, it is difficult to save money from monthly income, Even people who have a high monthly income suffer from financial problems as a result of wrong financial disposal and planning and personal loans to meet their needs.

The economic solidarity is one of the programs that provide liquidity to all community individuals. The program is divided into three sections: the first one is related to individuals through personal account, the second one is related to family through family account, making all the family individuals participate in saving liquidity, and the third one is for all community individuals through community individuals' solidarity by exerting efforts of major companies in such program, in order to access suitable solutions to get rid of financial problems.

This issue presents some solutions that will be explained in detail through many studies done on all the community groups, in addition to the most important results realized by such experiments and their efficient role in the avoidance of economic problems.

The programs to be discussed are as follows:

1. Personal solidarity program (personal account)

2. Family solidarity program (family account)

3. Social solidarity program

PERSONAL SOLIDARITY PROGRAM

Personal solidarity:

Economic analysts warned that middle class began to disappear all over the world, and some economic experts indicate that middle class is important in a community as it represents economic strength as a working and producing class. It is the source of economic, social, and political stability of community. In addition, it supports economy. Studies indicate that the middle class represents 13% of the total world population, and the middle class ratio increases in the advanced industrial countries, reaching 90% from the total population. Moreover, there are many factors causing the diminishing of the middle class worldwide. Some of these factors are as follows: the dependence totally on the bank facilities (personal loans) and individuals being not aware of the risk of such facilities. Accordingly, many borrowers are bound with the loans and their interests for a long period. The matter leads to deduction of high ratio of monthly income, and in turn, this can reflect on the level of living and family and social stability. And one of the implications is financial problems and exposure to poverty. Lastly, it is obvious that the faltering real estate contributions pending for long periods and phantom contributions represent the most important reasons leading to poverty recently. These cost a high volume of the savings of middle. The major effect of poverty on an individual, especially if he is responsible for a family, is that it leads to family problems and conflict or can lead to the refused surrender, which lastly leads to psychological collapse, interpreted as an inability to resist the poverty. In turn, his family causes pressures through their main requirements unlike accessories or even the emotional ones which they missed. He will be in front of two options: getting rid of either his life or his family.

Many middle class persons have a sufficient monthly income to cover all life requirements, but most of the income is used to acquire financial facilities from the banks. A recent study done in the Arabic world proves that the ratio of 93% from the middle class depend totally on the personal loans given by the bank to meet their needs. The matter leads to deduction of 36% from the monthly income to pay dues of the bank, and 67% of income is spent on invoices and foodstuff. Studies also prove that 89% of the middle class continue to get loan after loan if the bank is ready to refinance.

The matter causes financial problems to customers, which they cannot get rid of and may continue to the period after they finish their services in the governmental or private sector.

And now some methods formulated through studies and experiments related to the economic solidarity used by all community groups and the extent to which the methods can reduce financial problems are given.

Personal Solidarity Program Usage Method

According to an experiment, study was conducted on the middle class, the income of which ranges between 4000 and 8000 SR monthly. The said process makes the middle class personnel expressing their desire to join the personal solidarity program in order to save 37% yearly, and now we overview personal experiment details of an employee working in a private sector as given in

Table 1:

Name of employee	Ali Shady
Monthly salary	3500.00 (incoming amounts)
Type of accommodation	Rent
Renting charges	900.00 (outgoing amounts)
Electric bill	67.00 (outgoing amounts)
Vehicle installments	650.00 (outgoing amounts)
Net salary	1883.00 SR
Allocation of ratios	
Salary	10%
Personal loans	10%
Extras	10%

The above-mentioned employee has applied personal solidarity for 11 months (24 weeks) where he has daily deposited money in his private account, along with allocating 10% from the monthly income, the details of which are presented in Table 2.

Table 2:

Income	Weeks	Date		Amount	Extra	Source	Ratio	Balance	Available
3.500 SR	1	31/01	06/02	89	350	Salary	10%	439	439
	2	07/02	13/02	81	0	—	0	520	520
	3	14/02	02/02	79	0	—	0	599	599
	4	21/02	27/02	69	0	—	0	668	668
3,500 SR	5	28/02	06/03	77	350	Salary	10%	1,095	1,095
	6	07/03	13/03	167	0	0	0	1,262	1,262
	7	14/03	20/03	98	0			1,360	1,360
	8	21/03	27/03	44	0			1,404	1,404
3,500 SR	9	28/03	03/04	56	350	Salary	10%	1,810	1,810
	10	04/03	10/04	69	0			1,879	1,879
	11	11/04	17/04	108	0			1,987	1,987
	12	18/04	04/04	14	0			2,001	2,001
3,500 SR	13	25/04	01/05	98	350	Salary	10%	2,449	2,449
	14	02/05	08/05	57	0			2,506	2,506
	15	09/05	15/05	86	0			2,592	2,592
	16	16/05	22/05	56	0			2,648	2,648
	17	23/05	29/05	93	0			2,741	2,741
3,500 SR	18	30/05	05/06	189	350	Salary	10%	3,280	3,280
	19	06/06	12/06	65	0			3,345	3,345
	20	13/06	19/06	67	0			3,412	3,412
	21	20/06	26/06	78	0			3,490	3,490
3,500 SR	22	27/06	03/07	83	350	Salary	10%	3,923	3,923
	23	04/07	10/07	93	0			4,016	4,016
	24	11/07	17/07	56	0			4,072	4,072

Experiments Results

According to the account statement of the mentioned person, it is obvious that he earns 4.072 SR within six months, and the amount is considered as a factor supporting in the avoidance of long-term financial and bank facilities problems, whereas most of the people depend on personal loans for all their financial needs.

Family Solidarity Program

Family solidarity program (family account):

Family is the main component of community; it is the simple environment in which a human practices his life. Family should be kept and built to apply optimal principles, and the most dangerous thing the human faces is poverty, which can lead to many wrong behaviors committed by some people from the poor class. Such behaviors, which can result in crime with great impact, threaten security. The matter shall be rather risky if many families suffer from poverty. In that case, crime can spread as a result of the family (as a main component of community) suffering from poverty. Some most important crimes committed by such poor families are theft, trading of prohibited products, and practice of underworld. Mostly there may be drug dealers who exploit the poor family in promoting or smuggling drugs, especially adolescents and children, where it may be difficult for the father to control his family member and may surrender as a result of non-availability of other income.

The main cause of poverty and its spread is family disintegration and the separation of the person financially from his family, where many people receiving monthly income think that they are free to use his money without allowing anyone to know his financial situation details. This makes them independent, and they seek financial support through personal loans and bank facilities. Finally, they shall be forced to pay most of his monthly income towards the loans received from bank facilities and financing companies.

Family Solidarity Program Usage Method

A study was conducted on a number of families whose total income is 34.640 SR monthly applying personal solidarity program. The most important characteristic of such program is to provide an additional income, which can be utilized where needed. The details of the experiment are given in Table 3.

- The family members are nine (middle class).

Table 3: **Family monthly income details**

Name	Relation	Monthly income (SR)	Profession	Bank loan liabilities	Net
Sami	Paterfamilias	2,300	Retired	0,00	2,300
Sara	Wife	0,00	—	0	0
Mohammed	Son	1,150	Governmental allocations	0	1,150
Hamad	Son	10,000	Teacher	2,150	7,850
Saleh	Son	8,790	Security man	1,890	6,900
Fahad	Son	3,500	Customer service employee	0	3,500
Ahmed	Son	8,900	Security man	2,580	6,320
Hissa	Daughter	0,00	—	0	0
Hind	Daughter	0.0	—	0	0
Total		**34,640**		**6,620**	**28,020**

The above-mentioned family members allocate 15% from the monthly income for everyone as detailed in Table 4.

Table 4:

Name	Relation	Monthly income (SR)	Allocated ratio	Amount	Total
Sami	Paterfamilias	2.300	15%	345	345
Sara	Wife	0.00	—	0.00	—
Mohammed	Son	1.150	15%	172	517
Hamad	Son	10.000	10%	1.000	1.517
Saleh	Son	8.790	10%	879	2.317
Fahad	Son	3.500	15%	525	2.842
Ahmed	Son	8.900	10%	890	3.732
Hissa	Daughter	0.00	—	0.00	—
Hind	Daughter	0,00	—	0,00	—
Total		34,640	Net income		3,811

Experiment Result

The family members save 3.811 SR monthly and divide the amount among the members who have no monthly income (three members). Therefore, everyone earns 1.270 SR monthly as a bonus until they will find a suitable work.

SOCIAL SOLIDARITY PROGRAM

Solidarity means realization of social justice. The justifications of solidarity depend on the availability of a group of people facing shortage in all the financial and emotional requirements. The shortage forces them to deviate from the right path to meet their financial objectives. This deviation takes place when this group is ignored, and when this group commits offenses, the level of social security decreases, with cases of theft and murder increasing due to the desperate need for money, which people suffering from poverty and unemployment actually face.

Businessmen who own many trading establishments should utilize services from this group by employing them in their firms so that both parties mutually benefit from each other. This matter realizes the principles of social justice, which in turn makes the members of this community contributes to efficient community building as per their educational or cultural standard. **Nevertheless, according to their requirements the companies train people who apply for work, this means no one is required to submit his qualifications before training,** but because of the administrative corruption in some companies, they adhere to some conditions that not available for most of the applicants. The company also should specify certain period of time to train new employees to know the work requirements in order to realize the objectives.

Many businessmen who have huge wealth are exposed to the risk of theft either directly or indirectly by closer people, and mostly, such theft covers hundred millions deposited in accounts of persons who monopolize such money or, otherwise, may use it in illegal enterprises. Businessman may know that some of his money is stolen by one of his relatives or closer people in the work environment, but he keeps quiet for one of two reasons: Either he can punish him at the suitable time, or he has sufficient amount of liquidity as he thinks the theft shall not affect his financial position, and if all businessmen make accountability system for the monopolized money, many of the financial problems will disappear and communities get rid of monopoly.

Investors and businessmen are categorized into three sections:

First section: businessmen who have wealth estimated to milliards (from one milliard and over):

They often have several business activities; in addition, they have the ability to employ unemployed people, using them in the execution of business projects and distributing the tasks according to their educational standards. The businessmen who own large wealth should control and observe their account and protect them from monopoly, where the total amounts monopolized as a result of the absence of sufficient control reach 780 millions. The matter is sufficient to establish a company, the employees of which can be estimated to 16000, and accordingly, we conclude that the money monopoly is a main reason of unemployment and poverty, and the businessmen have a great role to get rid of this phenomenon.

Second section: businessmen having a wealth estimated to hundred millions (from 100 millions to 950 millions):

They have an ability to have the largest capital through establishing new branches in the same activity practiced by the establishment. Such new branches employ the unemployed people, where they will be trained to perform their work tasks along with dropping the experience condition which is difficult to be met by most of the applicants. We conclude that such establishments can account unemployed people through charging a teamwork to provide great amount of jobs exactly in the companies having greater treatment of customers.

Third section: businessmen having a wealth estimated to millions (from one million to 99 million Saudi riyals):

Such group of businessmen have a sufficient ability to use unemployed people in the execution of some projects (small investors). When this group finds sufficient liquidity, this means that economy is stable, where the expansion of this group activity indicates the decline of financial problems, increase of employment for graduates, and decreasing ratio of unemployment. It is known when the activity of the company expands, it needs a large number of employees, **accordingly, small and medium-size establishments susceptible to bankruptcy, but they will be supported by businessmen who shall reveal their an efficient participation.**

Important Advices for Companies and Establishments

The reason for a company's bankruptcy is the decline of customer desire as a result of low quality of product and customer service. This means when the product is of high quality, customer desires to buy. This encourages the producing company to establish new branches depending on the increasing demand; accordingly, this establishment realizes the social solidarity program and hires unemployed people and employs them in the new branches.

Social Solidarity Program Usage Method

This method depends on four main steps. Each one is integral part:

First step: businessmen allocate 1% from the capital as per the following schedule as detailed in Table 5.

Table 5:

Companies	Trading activity	Capital	Ratio allocated to the fund (1%)	Total
Company 1	Contracting and maintenance	350.000.000	3.500.000	3.500.000
Company 2	Foodstuff	460.000.000	4.600.000	8.100.000
Company 3	Restaurant group	11.000.000	110.000	8.210.00
Company 4	Furniture exhibition	190.000.000	1.900.000	10.110.000
Company 5	Home furniture	24.000.000	240.000	10.350.000
Company 6	Real estate	10.000.000	100.000	10.450.000
Company 7	Telecommunication	8.000.000	80.000	10.530.000
Company 8	Computer maintenance	21.000.000	210.000	10.740.000
Company 9	Furniture installment	18.000.000	180.000	10.920.000
Company 10	General services	15.000.000	150.000	11.070.000

Second step: Collecting such contributions amount to 11.070.000 millions. This amount (capital) is sufficient to establish an organization with the capital earned from the businessmen contributions.

Third step: Determining the company trading activity and completing all procedures required by the governmental departments to begin practicing such trading activity, in addition to furnishing the company site and providing all the facilities required.

Fourth step: Advertising vacant, available jobs giving preferences to the applicants who have not been recruited before, in order to avoid employing people who are working at specified organization and receiving high salaries but searching for the best financial situations. This group should be avoided in order to appoint unemployed ones.

Fifth step: Shares are distributed among businessmen as per their contribution, where the nominal value is 10 SR, and profits will be distributed in accordance with the ownership ratio for every shareholder.

Schedule (6-1)

Such schedule explains the number of unemployed people who are included in this study from 19/7/2010 to 12/5/2012 in a number of Arab and Gulf countries along with describing their scientific qualifications and majors:

Scientific degree	Major	Number of unemployed	Country	Reasons of unemployment
Doctorate		21,900		Non-availability of vacancy
Master		34,987	Saudi Arabia, Kuwait	Full dependence on expats
Bachelor		109,432	Bahrain, Egypt, Qatar	Administrative corruption
Diploma	All majors	198,094	Syria, Sudan, Yemen	Increasing number of graduates
High school		343,098	Lebanon, Algeria, Tunisia	Absence of job-administrative organization
Intermediate		210,154	Libya, Jordan, Emirates	Money monopoly
Low-level certificate		92,430		Company bankruptcy

One of the establishments advertises 250 vacant jobs in different majors. After advertising, the applicants were 10.987, and statistics indicate the applicants represent 18% from the total population of city in which this establishment is located. Such advertisement—the contents of which stipulate vacant jobs—explains the actual number of unemployed who are available in the area of the advertising establishment.

Experiment Results

If every ten businessmen cooperate in solidarity to establish an organization to employ a large number of unemployed people and increase their profits as per their contributions in such organization, we reach the following results:

1. Diminishing number of unemployed people.

2. Enhancing economies of businessmen and expanding their trading activities in a manner that serves the general benefit.

3. Utilizing abilities of unemployed and poor-class people in establishing many projects, where a private program will be prepared to train such group of people to work in such organizations as required.

4. Decreasing level of bankruptcy companies threatened with insolvency. The participation of each company in the solidarity program preserves its financial & economic position and becomes out of risks

Conclusion

Money is a basic need for all. The amount of money needed for individuals or groups varies according to their lifestyle. All people are keen to earn money in order to meet their life requirements. In addition, the individuals and families included in this program (economic solidarity) supported themselves in decreasing their financial shortage and getting rid of financial problems. If they find an additional income, they can use it at a suitable time.

Therefore, businessmen shall contribute to the economic solidarity program, where the role of the businessmen is to removes the hurdles from which unemployed and poor class suffers. This issue, which includes some solutions suit some groups of community, is of high importance in this field.

Lastly, I hope this issue shall be of high benefit and be appreciated by all, at the time. The coming issues will discuss many solutions studied in the field of economy, and the coming program will be (Fighting Company Bankruptcy and Individual Financial Problems) for the banks and companies who wish to use such program. For further information about such program and the most important achievements of the author, please visit the following site:

www.authormhalzahrani.org

praise be upon him

Most references from sites on the Internet

Three box

www.authoralzahrani.org

Prepared by

Mohammed Al Zahrani

Review & coordination

Raid Mohammed Bugis

Translate by

Professional Translation Office

INDEX

T

theft   24, 29-31

U

unemployment   29, 32-3, 37

V

vacant jobs, stipulate   38

W

wealth   30-2

www.ingramcontent.com/pod-product-compliance
Lightning Source LLC
Chambersburg PA
CBHW021938170526
45157CB00005B/2335